i am THE Other WOMAN

CONFESSIONS OF A BLACK, EDUCATED, PROFESSIONAL CHRISTIAN

Teira E. Farley

i am The Other Woman:
Confessions of a Black, Educated, Professional Christian

Copyright © 2024 by Teira E. Farley

All rights reserved. Printed in the United States of America. No part of this book may be used or reproduced in any manner whatsoever without written permission except in the case of brief quotations embodied in critical articles or reviews.

For information, please visit teiraefarley.com

All scripture quotations, unless otherwise indicated, are taken from The Holy Bible, King James Version, which is public domain. Scripture quotations marked ESV are taken from the ESV® (The Holy Bible, English Standard Version®). Copyright © 2001 by Crossway, a publishing ministry of Good News Publishers. Used by permission. All rights reserved.

Published by epiphany thecoloringbox.com

ISBN: 979-8-9914863-8-5

First Edition: February 2022

Dedication

To my mother,

Thank you for always seeing the other woman in me ...
not perfect, but exactly as He created me to be.

P.S. You were right. It is totally okay to write your prayers down :).

"Our deepest fear is not that we are inadequate. Our deepest fear is that we are powerful beyond measure. It is our light, not our darkness that most frightens us. We ask ourselves, Who am I to be brilliant, gorgeous, talented, fabulous? Actually, who are you not to be? You are a child of God. Your playing small does not serve the world. There is nothing enlightened about shrinking so that other people won't feel insecure around you. We are all meant to shine, as children do. We were born to make manifest the glory of God that is within us. It's not just in some of us; it's in everyone. And as we let our own light shine, we unconsciously give other people permission to do the same. As we are liberated from our own fear, our presence automatically liberates others."

- Marianne Williamson, A Return to Love: Reflections on the Principles of a Course in Miracles[1]

FOREWORD

Chances are, you've heard the many "self" words. There's self-esteem, self-acceptance, self-respect, self-confidence, self-love, self-care, and so on. There are so many words to describe how we feel about ourselves, how we think about ourselves, and how we act toward ourselves. It's understandable if they all start to blend together for you; however, they are indeed different concepts with unique meanings, findings, and purposes intended for you to seek deeper into your existence.

In this masterpiece, *"i am The Other Woman,"* you will find detailed *confessions of a black, educated, professional christian*, which will not only help you show more grace and kindness to yourself, but will also elevate your prayer life, improve your self-compassion, and help you realize your worth in the sight of God. Clearly, many of the *confessions* shared are applied confirmations, deeply immersed in the concept of who God has created you to be.

Ephesians 2:10, ESV, states *"For we are his workmanship, created in Christ Jesus for good works, which God prepared beforehand, that we should walk in them."*

Teira E. Farley speaks to the body, soul, and spirit of all women. Regardless of race, religion, or beliefs, Teira unveils the truth, which is found by embracing the complete picture of who we really are. It's not necessary to have a high sense of self-confidence in every area of your life; there are naturally some things that you will simply not be very good at, and other areas, in which, you will excel. The important thing is to have self-confidence in the activities in your life that matter to YOU and openly declare *confessions* of a high sense of self-worth, overall.

The challenges and constant changes of life are both internal and external. Women are forced to multitask in an inconsistent world, thus an inconsistent culture complicated with the pressures of society. This book is a road map designed to help you navigate your journey with enthusiasm, tenacity, and dedication. It's through prayer, faith, and trust that you will develop new thoughts, new opinions, and gain a new perception of the valuable "workmanship" you are.

Seeing all of yourself is important and vital to your holistic fulfillment. This book is a great step in helping you move in that direction.

- JaNean Stubbs-Taylor

CONTENTS

INTRODUCTION

CONFESSION I.	i am A MASTERPIECE	3
CONFESSION II.	i am SAVED	5
CONFESSION III.	i am CHOSEN	7
CONFESSION IV.	i am FAITHFUL	9
CONFESSION V.	i am GRACEFULLY BROKEN	11
CONFESSION VI.	i am NOT CRAZY	13
CONFESSION VII.	i am SECURE	15
CONFESSION VIII.	i am PATIENT	17
CONFESSION IX.	i am INTELLIGENT	19
CONFESSION X.	i am POWERFUL	21
CONFESSION XI.	i am BEAUTIFUL	23
CONFESSION XII.	i am SENSUAL & SEXUAL	25
CONFESSION XIII.	i am A DAUGHTER	27
CONFESSION XIV.	i am A SISTER	29
CONFESSION XV.	i am A WIFE	31

CONFESSION XVI.	i am A MOTHER	33
CONFESSION XVII.	i am A FRIEND	35
CONFESSION XVIII.	i am AN INTERCESSOR	37
CONFESSION XIX.	i am A SERVANT	39
CONFESSION XX.	i am A STUDENT	41
CONFESSION XXI.	i am AN EDUCATOR	43
CONFESSION XXII.	i am A PROFESSIONAL	45
CONFESSION XXIII.	i am AN ENTREPRENEUR	47
CONFESSION XXIV.	i am A CREATIVE	49
CONFESSION XXV.	i am A CHAMPION	51
CONFESSION XXVI.	i am HEALTHY	53
CONFESSION XXVII.	i am WHOLE	55
CONFESSION XXVIII.	i am WORTHY	57
CONFESSION XXIX.	i am FREE	59
CONFESSION XXX.	i am HAPPY	61
CONFESSION XXXI.	i am LOVED	63
CONFESSION XXXII.	i am ENOUGH	65
CONFESSION XXXIII.	i am THE OTHER WOMAN	67
A CHARGE TO BE	JAMETTA CHANDLER MOORE	69

INTRODUCTION

Disclaimer: If you had your heart set on a juicy, tell-all novel filled with real accounts of secrets from the eyes of someone living a double life, then keep reading. You may be on to something, but it's not what you think...

By the way, this book is in no way, shape or form an admission to or condoning of affairs, adultery, lying, cheating, denial, betrayal, or deception. Be encouraged.

Confessions. Not Affirmations.

Why? Simple. Before you can affirm a thing, you must first confirm it to be so.

I believe people, women particularly, struggle with positive affirmations because we haven't first paused to acknowledge and embrace the fullness and totality of who we are. We purpose our lives in everyone and everything outside of ourselves, all the while ignoring the introspective pieces that ultimately yield the inner peace and satisfaction we're seeking. We slip into boxes formed by others' definitions and expectations, or we hide in their shadows. We minimize our intellect and opinions to conform to societal, demographic, and gender norms. We dilute our opinions to appease the comfort of professional superiors and coworkers. We suppress and internalize our struggles because we don't want to be mislabeled or mishandled. We project our insecurities on to others to avoid reviewing the reflection of what we see, feel, and believe within. More often than not, we battle ... silently.

This book is a tool to unlock the "other" parts of your existence. This time, it's not about "them"; it's about you. What you did or didn't do before this point in time is no longer relevant. When something happened or what once was can no longer be your focus. This moment is an open invitation for you to confess, believe, and change as YOU see fit.

A transformation of this nature begins with a thought, a belief, a concept that you recognize and later accept. Reshaping your perspective and redefining your truth will prompt you to implement actions, which will manifest the reality you once envisioned and most importantly, the one God originally ordained.

I welcome you to adjust your mindset regarding who you are and who you can be. Recognize this list of confessions is not intended to be all inclusive or all encompassing. All areas may not apply to you. That's perfectly fine. I'm merely offering a starting point for you to evaluate what may be missing from your mind, heart, or spirit, so you can posture yourself to live beyond these self-imposed limitations. Read the confessions one by one, in pairs, or grouped together. Regardless of your preference, be sure to read with intention, carefully processing, and releasing all inhibitions as you go.

Take time to reflect. Examine your behaviors. Learn new patterns. Institute better habits. Claim your healing. Pursue wholeness. Reject fear. Choose freedom. Accept all of your attributes as they are, your strengths, your weaknesses, and everything in between. Dig deeper, so you can go higher. Champion what makes you uniquely you.

Yes, you are *The Other Woman*. It's time for you to identify and awaken the other side(s) of you. Don't be intimidated by your brilliance. Embark upon this voyage to learn more about yourself, and then pray over your newfound discovery to ensure you never lose that(those) part(s) of you again.

Life is about choices. You live. You learn. You grow. You evolve. You become. Throughout this process, you are often exposed to situations and circumstances that are less than desirable. You are left hurt, rejected, abandoned, disgruntled, frustrated, saddened, and confused. In those moments, you often retreat to what's comfortable or what you've stored in your mental Rolodex of "proper" responses. While in some cases, that may be best or seem appropriate, there are other times when you are perpetuating bad habits, and preserving debilitating, unhealthy thought patterns.

Somewhere along the lines, you either stopped believing in who you were created to be, or you realized that you never fully tapped into all of it in the first place. The goal is simple: embrace every facet of yourself just as God has. He saw a void, so He created you to fill it. When you don't foster your unique value, you're basically telling God He got it wrong or fell short on His execution. Shrinking into a fraction of yourself or fighting to become someone else is insulting to your creator and degrading to your destiny. God deserves the best you have to offer because He gave you the capacity to be just that, the best. An appropriate expression of gratitude is to honor Him daily. You do that by celebrating the works of His hands, and reveling in ALL of the ingredients that comprise the recipe that is you.

Awaken the other side of you, that part you've been hiding and shying away from. It is all a portion of His masterpiece and deserves to be shared with the world. Your ignorance, pride, and stubbornness can't even keep Him away.

Invite God to help. He's the most equipped for the job. Not sure how?

Let us pray.

i am A MASTERPIECE

Father, thank You for the gift of life.

Thank You for the activity of my limbs, for keeping me in my right mind, for making me a vessel filled with love, purpose, and empathy. You had an idea of who I would be and what I could accomplish. You thought it was good, so You spoke me into existence. Don't allow circumstances to overwhelm me and cause me to forget that fact. Father, forgive me for not always walking in the fullness of who You created me to be. Anoint my mind to filter out thoughts that are not of You. Consume my spirit that it might be guided to fulfill Your purpose in the Earth. Dominate my being so that each decision I make is representative of Your kingdom. Grant me favor, direction, and creativity that I might not wander unnecessarily. When I get distracted, grab my attention. When I doubt my abilities, remind me that I am fashioned after You. When I feel the weight is unbearable or that I have to face it all alone, evoke Your presence in me to show me that I have access to You. When I feel defeated, revitalize me. Connect me to people who know You and can see me, even those who recognize more in me than I may currently see in myself. Stir up gifts and skills in me that are currently lying dormant. Give me the desires of my heart so I may contrive my wish list from that which pleases You. Align my actions with Your will. Create in me a clean heart and renew the right spirit in me. Don't allow my living, my praying, my working, my reading, my learning, or my teaching to be in vain. Show me how to embrace who I am as Your original creation, without alteration or expectation for change. Shatter distractions, doubt, and fear that attempt to disconnect me from You. Nurture me in Your likeness that I might become exactly who You envisioned me to be. Because of You, i am a masterpiece.

In Jesus' name, Amen.

God is patient. He's kind. He's gentle. He is filled with warmth and solicitude, generosity, and understanding. So much so, He put a plan in place to cover your mistakes and forgive your sins long before you made them. He sacrificed the life of His son, our Lord and Savior, Jesus Christ, to atone for our sins. The only thing He asks is that you choose Him, choose to be free, in Him, today and forevermore. He gave you an option to be forgiven, delivered, and then live with Him for eternity. Your responsibility is to believe in Him. He doesn't force himself upon you, but places you in environments that allow for an introduction to His presence, His grace, His strength, His power, His wisdom, His peace, His sustenance, His companionship, and ultimately, His love.

The most beautiful thing about having a relationship with God is that there is nothing you can do to mess it up. He is not thrown off of His throne by your shortcomings and failures. Your mistakes don't catch Him off guard. On the contrary, He's always there to remind you that you can overcome anything, and be better, if you rely on Him more than yourself.

Uncovering the other part(s) of you begins with knowing whose you are and making a decision to dedicate your life to aligning with His will. He is patiently waiting to show you who you are. Having a solid, strong relationship with God is the tie that binds your life together with purpose and fulfillment. It's a joy knowing that you've got the undefeated champion of the world in your corner, speaking to you, guiding you, covering you, healing you, and pushing you to conquer your fears and accomplish your goals. He wants you to stay on the right side of right and He's availed himself to make sure you have all you need to make that happen.

Let us pray.

i am SAVED

Father, thank You for introducing Yourself to me.

Thank You for surrounding me with people who know You, those who love You, and those who fully acknowledge You as their savior. Thank You for speaking to me, for calling me, for choosing me as Yours. Thank You for forgiving me of all of my sins, both known and unknown. Thank You for assisting me with living a life that would serve as a beacon of light to others. Father, forgive me for not always walking in the fullness of who You created me to be. Continue to fill me with a knowledge of Your will with all wisdom and spiritual understanding. Show me where I am to go in You. Show me the life You desire me to lead. Endow me with Your spirit to guide my footsteps and each of my decisions. Speak to me to keep me on the right path. Allow me to be an example of Your love in my community, and ultimately, the world. Allow my words to speak life and bring healing to the broken, insight to the confused, joy to the downtrodden, and peace to the disturbed. Help me to learn from my mistakes and silence the judgment of the enemy in my ear. Show me how to be an encourager, an influencer, and an inspiration. Protect me from traps that would be detrimental to my development as Your brand ambassador. Shield me from distractions that would pull me away from You or out of communion with Your spirit. Regardless of the moves I make, don't take Your hand off of my life. When I fall, teach me, forgive me, redirect me, and restore me. Remind me of the initial reasons You saved me. Use me to bring others to You, so they might feel Your love, Your gentleness, Your grace, and Your peace. Show me how to bring honor to the lifestyle of the believer. Fulfill Your purpose in my life this day and forevermore. Because of You, i am saved.

In Jesus' name, Amen.

Out of all of the people in the world, God chose you. He perfected your smile. He fashioned your style. He crafted your speech. He deposited your quirky habits, your competitive nature, ironic tastes, sarcasm, and sense of humor; or, He decided they didn't fit you well and held them for someone else. He granted you intellect to process thoughts and communicate with others, sometimes even on His behalf. He wrote your story, from beginning to end, giving you everything you would need to become everything you would want to be. He built you to win, to overcome, to excel, and to soar.

It is easy to allow disappointments to cloud your judgment, to be crippled by fear and doubt, tormented by thoughts that plague your mind and cause you to over analyze past decisions, or wonder if you even have what it takes to get the job done. Am I enough? Will I get this right? What will people say? Questions of this nature fill our minds and consume us with trepidation and discouragement.

In times of uncertainty, call up your faith and nudge yourself to remember you were not only created by Him, in His image, but you were also chosen for a reason, or two, or ten, to do a thing, or twelve, or twenty. He pre-approved you. Before you were born, He understood ALL of you. He introduced you into existence because there was something He wanted you to do. Your decisions can't qualify you for His presence any more than they can disqualify you from His power, His glory, or His splendor. He brought you into the world to be a representation of Him and His kingdom. The only way to get the details of your assignment(s) is to tap into His voice. Allow His spirit to guide your heart and mind as you make decisions on a day-to-day basis. Wondering how to do it?

Let us pray.

i am CHOSEN

Father, thank You for selecting me.

Thank You for distinguishing me from the masses. Thank You for giving me a unique purpose and assignment, despite the availability of alternative options. Thank You for perfecting my abilities so that I might effectively and productively complete the tasks You've prescribed. Thank You for allowing me to be a carrier of Your glory. Thank You for pursuing me and showing me how special I am. Father, forgive me for not always walking in the fullness of who You created me to be. In times of discontent and restlessness, remind me of the value I carry. In times of confusion, show me why You chose me. Strengthen me for the journey ahead. Build my support system with people who recognize my skills, talents, and capabilities, but aren't intimidated or blinded by them. Allow them to see my greatness as an asset, not a liability. Don't allow my networks and connections to block access to those who are in need of what I have to offer. Search my heart and remove anything that is not like You. Lord, You called me to be brave, to blaze trails, to open doors, to build, to elevate, and to evoke change. Don't allow me to get comfortable. Grant me an authentic connection with You so I can continually evolve as You desire. Don't let fame or fortune create distance between us. If an invention is needed, download it into my spirit. If a word needs to be spoken, prompt me to say it. Please allow the words of my mouth and the meditations of my heart to continue to be acceptable in Your sight. You are my strength, and You are my redeemer. Most importantly, God, don't allow me to make You regret Your choice. Don't ever give up on me and choose another. I am Your servant; I will obey. I am open, willing, and available to serve Your will. Because of You, i am chosen.

In Jesus' name. Amen.

Doubt. Fear. Confusion. Rejection. Disappointment. Hearing those words automatically trigger negative thoughts and emotions. They may even remind you of some of your lowest moments and the most discouraging of circumstances. It's okay. Pretending like you won't be tested in your beliefs after committing your life to God is ludicrous, teetering on the border of insanity.

Life will bring challenges. It's inevitable. What is debatable is how you respond to them, the level of power and control you yield to them, and what steps You take to navigate in, through, and around them. You have to remind yourself of your inner strength, your resilience, and the resolute power divinely bestowed upon you during your creation. Faith is not about pretending that nothing is bothering you. Suppressing your emotions isn't healthy and will not yield beneficial, holistic, long-lasting, or positive results. Faith is an internal belief system that charges and recharges you based upon the understanding that despite what is happening, better is possible.

Think about your last trial, the unexpected betrayal, or that horrifying experience that dropped you down to your knees, broke your heart, or completely discouraged your spirit. Now look around you. Take in a deep breath and release it. Examine the present moment. Completely acknowledge that you are on the other side of that situation. You made it! By the grace of God, you made it. If He healed you before, if He forgave you before, if He opened up a door before, then He can absolutely do it again. The burden of proof and the responsibility to perform lies in the hands of the Almighty. Your sole responsibility is to believe. Allow your memory to fuel your faith. His resume is beyond impressive, and the best part about it? You don't have to check for a reference; you are one.

Let us pray.

i am FAITHFUL

Father, thank You for my belief in You.

Thank You for the seeds of faith that were sown before I was born. Thank You for birthing me into a family of people who believe in You, emphatically, and love You, without reservation. Thank You for raising me in a household of faith. If I came to know You without familial influences, thank You for meeting me where I was and for building my foundation solely in You. Regardless of time and tenure, thank you for the inherent depth of my developing relationship with You. Thank You for intriguing me, pricking my intellect, evoking my curiosity, and teaching me that my belief in You is a tool to be revered, not a burden to be hidden. Father, forgive me for not always walking in the fullness of who You created me to be. As I continue to build my life as a believer, don't allow me to become weary in well doing. Don't permit negativity to quench my thirst for You. Immerse me in experiences that will strengthen my belief system. Prepare me for them. Bolster my self-confidence with Your identity. Teach me how to properly channel my energy and my efforts to continually refine and redefine who I am based upon Your instructions, not the validation or applause of others. Show me how to be intentional and deliberate about my walk with You. Provide me with resources, study guides, healthy connections, and insightful experiences that intensify my faith. Teach me proper perspective, so I am not deterred by failure, but rather propelled, shaped, and molded by it. Allow my faith to show me how to fail forward, not to be misled by ambition, clout, or material things. Grant me continual regeneration in You as I go after the life, relationships, and responsibilities, you have so graciously placed within my reach. Because of You, i am faithful.

In Jesus' name, Amen.

At some point in time, you were hurt. It could have been by a parent, a sibling, a classmate, an educator, a coach, or a friend. The deeper the connection between you and the individual, the harder it was to overcome the pain and anguish of the situation.

May I share something with you? That didn't disqualify you from anything. God didn't throw you away because someone mishandled you. In many cases, their words and actions were more of a representation of what they lacked, not what you were in need of. People tend to project their insecurities and inhibitions onto others. Unfortunately, you may have been the victim of their deficiencies.

But what if that isn't the case? What if you did exactly what they said, and you are exactly who they asserted? So. What. Forgive yourself and move on. Don't hold your life and evolution in bondage because of a temporary lapse of judgment or a fleeting moment of immature behavior. You are more than the sum of your mistakes and the results of your mishaps.

Did it ever occur to you that perhaps each of those situations contributed to the beauty you behold today? Maybe you now have a more compassionate perspective of others, or maybe you aren't as quick to make judgments, or hold a grudge, or insert yourself, unnecessarily (and often uninvited), into things that don't concern you. Whatever the case, regardless of the depth or the origin of the scar, it is uniquely yours. It is a part of your story and your testimony. Own it. Embrace it. Share it. You never know who will be blessed or empowered by it. Most importantly, if you remain stuck in the residue of your past, you will never enjoy your future, or the freedom and progression garnered by your acceptance.

Let us pray.

i am GRACEFULLY BROKEN

Father, thank You for my experiences.

Without You, I am nothing, yet with You, there is nothing I cannot do. You are my fortress. You are my strong tower. You are my protection. You are my shield. You can number the hairs on my head. You understand my thought patterns, my idiosyncrasies, my shortcomings, and my blind spots. You know the situations that will trip me up before they even occur. You identify the strongholds before they form; yet, you love me still, when I succumb to them. Father, forgive me for not always walking in the fullness of who You created me to be. Teach me how to emulate Your behavior. Teach me how to forgive myself. Teach me how to bounce back. Ignite the overcomer within me. Energize the conqueror I was predestined to be. Don't allow me to doubt myself. Reconcile my losses so that I approach future situations from the proper point of view. Shape my mind to appropriately filter and evaluate situations according to Your lens. Show me how not to hide under the guise of comfort or the shadow of expectations. Reveal intent. Reveal purpose. Reveal direction. Reveal strategy. Prompt me to ask the right questions so I can assess the roots of insecurity and pain. Spare me of false truths. Craft my story according to the uniqueness of my conditions, and show me how to embrace them along my journey. Allow me to see the beauty in my brokenness. Prepare me for success as You define it for my life. Dismiss distractions and eliminate excuses. Remind me that my healing is only offensive to people who benefit from my fragmented state, so their discontent with my progress is neither my concern nor my responsibility. Seal my evolution with the sanctity of Your spirit, the dominion of Your presence, and the authority of the cross. Because of You, i am gracefully broken.

In Jesus' name, Amen.

It happened. For whatever reason, God allowed it to be so. You're still breathing and obviously still coherent to some degree because you're reading a book. This tells me (and should serve as undeniable proof to you) that whatever was attempting to prevent you from moving forward has not won. The battle is not over and neither is the war. You haven't lost yet. You don't have to surrender. Despite how you're feeling or how you've felt, you are not a victim of your circumstances. You are not a prisoner to your past. You are not bound to or by your previous dreams or ambitions. You cannot control everything that happens to you, but you do possess the ability to determine how you will respond in various situations. You can decide today, right now, to do something different, and thus, yield an alternative, more desirable outcome.

Uncertainty is not indicative of a lack of intellect or sanity. On the contrary, indecision is often a result of an influx of information and processing overload. You're unable to make a decision because you've been presented with a myriad of options and alternatives and you've yet to determine which will yield the preferred results. You may feel crippled or unsure of yourself, but that is when you must dig into the root of those emotions so that you can address the problem at the source. Isolation may feel safe, but may not be what's best. If you don't possess what's needed to peel back those layers, ask for help, seek guidance, and work to gain clarity regarding your situation. This is a perfect opportunity to tap into your relationship with the Father. God is not the author of confusion, so whenever you find yourself amid havoc or mayhem, take a step back, retrace your steps, and figure out how you got there. You'll be amazed at what you find and equally encouraged to discover who was there with you the entire time, ready, willing, and available to guide you out of turmoil and into destiny.

Let us pray.

i am **NOT CRAZY**

Father, thank You for my sanity and my peace.

In the midst of chaos, confusion, and circumstances beyond my control, it is easy to feel overwhelmed. It can be alluring, even beguiling to succumb to the pressures of the world and begin to challenge if I even hear You at all. In those moments, whisper words of affirmation in my ear, or place me on someone's mind so they can reach out to me on Your behalf. Let me never forget that You created me for a specific purpose, which means I am well able to complete it. I must trust and always believe that if You gave me the vision, You will also create the path to secure the provision needed to bring it to fruition. Father, forgive me for not always walking in the fullness of who You created me to be. Remind me to look to You for assistance, direction, rejuvenation, courage, strength, and comfort. Teach me how to ignore negative influences and help ensure I don't become one. Show me how to fortify my faith with Your word. Surround me with people who have a strong sense of discernment and can hear beyond the words I speak. Silence uncertainty, worry, anxiety, panic, and self-elimination. Infiltrate my thought patterns with positive vibes, wisdom, faith, love, perseverance, trust, honor, respect, and patience. As You grant me grace, teach me how to extend it to myself. Allow Your favor to consume my errors, deficiencies, and imperfections so much so that even my failures transport me onward each time. Keep me from feeling isolated or believing I am the only one who is dealing with the troubles I face. Don't allow those troubles to overshadow my competence, my dexterity, or my genius. Stabilize my emotions and separate feelings from facts, allowing truth to prevail, and my security and tranquility to rest and abide solely and completely in you. Because of You, i am not crazy.

In Jesus' name, Amen.

When did it begin? Who told you that something was wrong with you? What was it that shattered your belief in humanity and made you question if God is real or why He allowed *this* to happen to *you*? Maybe it was the cancer diagnosis or the loss of your child. Perhaps it was when he broke off the engagement, in a Facebook post no less, or when you learned your older sister is your biological mother, meaning the mother you know is actually your grandmother. Do you think it was that moment from your childhood? You know, the one you never spoke of? Or maybe you did tell someone, and they either blamed you or acted as if it never occurred?

Whatever it was, whoever it involved, regardless of how much time has passed, it stole something from you. It birthed a narrative within you that has altered how you show up in the world. Your view of life is jaded, biased, and guarded. Keeping those memories and feelings suppressed is eating you alive. You're defensive, tormented, embarrassed, and defeated. You believe being cold, brash, and insulting is the only way to survive. You have an "I'll get them before they get me" mentality. You run away from thought provoking, revealing conversations. You shun vulnerability. You chastise fear as weakness. You reject emotion and affection, of any kind, from any source, but not because you don't desire it. You do so because you don't know how to welcome the unknown.

As ugly as it may have been, in many cases, the only person still reckoning with your past is you. Your life is currently based upon instability and insecurity. You don't trust in anything and it is costing you everything.

Don't empower the negativity another moment. You are not feeble or frail. Quit selling yourself on the worthless ideology that you don't need anyone. You do and it's okay. More than anything, you need God.

Let us pray.

i am SECURE

Father, thank You for confidence and divine protection.

Thank you for seeing me, all of me, and loving me in spite of. Thank you for treasuring my voice and my significance. Thank you for setting a standard and an example for how I should love and celebrate myself. Father, forgive me for not always walking in the fullness of who You created me to be. Sometimes I underestimate my importance. Sometimes, I don't get it right. I overthink. I procrastinate. I obsess over perfection. I disregard information that I should hold dear. I allow others to improperly influence me. I cling to events and negative experiences that I should yield to You and heal from. Despite my actions or inactions, in every situation, You are there. Thank You. Thank You for showing me that I can go forward even when it seems as if all of the odds are stacked against me. You know the inner parts of me. You know my intentions. You know my motives. You understand how I communicate. You know I am earnestly trying to please You. You also know I am my biggest critic. It is easy to crumble under the pressure of expectations, mine and others'. Grant me patience and understanding, trust and reliance in You. Teach me not to attempt to hide myself or my issues from You, but instead, to run to You with them. As you forgive me, teach me how to forgive others earnestly, completely, without keeping record, or storing up ammunition for future use. People will betray me or mishandle me. Some knowingly, others unknowingly, but don't let seeds of doubt and disappointment hinder my ability to embark upon future relationships. Release me from that trauma. Remind me that I don't have to condone their behavior to love and care about them, just as my issues have never jeopardized or forfeited Your love and care for me. Because of You, i am secure.

In Jesus' name, Amen.

Imagine being at a birthday party. Before you blow out the candles and spread germs all over the beautiful cake you were planning to share with family and friends, you close your eyes and make a wish. How different would your life be, if when you opened your eyes, your request had been granted? Imagine if the dream car was sitting in the driveway, a notice popped up on your phone acknowledging a direct deposit in the amount of your new bi-weekly salary, the offer letter was in your inbox, or the keys to your dream home were magically in your hand. How much more intentional would you be about your prayers if you knew that the moment you conceived the thought, there was no waiting period, but rather, the vision became an instant reality? Sounds amazing, right?

But what about those times when you prayed in anger or out of sheer frustration? What if those wishes you mumbled under your breath when you were a child took place instantly and there was no turning back? How many people would be injured, sick, or even dead? How much harm and damage would you have caused in moments of impatience or utter ignorance? Exactly.

Sometimes, the wait, although seemingly inconvenient and unyielding, is for your good. Time often offers insight. Beyond a proper view, time yields maturity and growth. Just like food tastes better when it marinates before it's cooked, your blessings will fit better when they are tailored to your specifications. Good things take time.

Don't despise the wait. Embrace it. Maximize it. Utilize it for personal development and proper preparation. Channel it as momentum and use it to evaluate probability and possibility. Allow it to help you better navigate your interactions, with others and yourself.

Let us pray.

CONFESSION VIII

i am PATIENT

Father, thank You for each breath that I breathe.

Focusing on my breaths reminds to slow down. Inhaling peace and exhaling anxiety allows me to take my time, to live in the present. Thank You for those subtle reminders to direct my attention to the things I can control and release the things that I cannot. Thank You for teaching me that gratitude changes perspective, that remaining in a position of admiration somehow makes the mountains look more like molehills. It is easy to be distracted when things aren't going as I planned or anticipated, to become despondent and discontent. Thank You for not giving up on me in those moments, but instead, exuding the very behavior you desire for me to emulate. Father, forgive me for not always walking in the fullness of who You created me to be. Teach me how to filter things through Your lens, remembering that everyone is going through something, whether I know of it or not. Keep potential and compassion in the forefront of my mind to help me withhold judgment from others. Remind me that it doesn't cost me anything to be kind, sincere, polite, and encouraging. Lord, remove the hesitation, distress, apprehension, and consternation that comes during the waiting periods. Teach me that sometimes, silence is a part of the process. Don't allow me to throw in the towel prematurely. Don't allow the enemy to trick me into thinking a lack of change, in any situation, is an indication of what will always be. Silence the voices that will send me into mental anguish and get me caught up in worrying about scenarios that only exist in my head. In the midst of it all, teach me how to wait well, taking full advantage of the additional space and opportunity to prepare. When the time finally comes for "it" to happen, make it worth the wait. Because of You, i am patient.

In Jesus' name, Amen.

There is a common adage that we hear in churches across the country and households of faith, both near and far. It is: what we do is only for Christ. While this may be true to an extent, what we often fail to acknowledge is that, more than being for Christ, what we do is of and from Christ. He created us as He determined necessary. He implanted a purpose and an assignment within our being from the onset. He bestowed gifts upon us and within us. He fashioned our ability to receive and process information, to regulate data, and even to make decisions independent of Him. We have the ability to interpret and execute based upon our measure of cognizance and understanding, all because He decided it to be so.

How we navigate various spaces and approach various scenarios is largely predicated upon how we view ourselves and the power we ascribe to our own voice. That power can be fueled by negativity and ignorance just as easily as it can be grounded in positivity and intellect.

It's important that we feed our minds as often as we feed our bodies and our spirits. Pretending we aren't as smart as we truly are, limiting our conversations to avoid being stereotyped, diminishing our contributions to accommodate the ego and pride of our counterparts, supervisors, friends, or family is counterintuitive to God's original intention and counterproductive to His ultimate goal of expanding His kingdom.

Resist the temptation to dumb down, mask, overshadow, or pull away from ALL of who you are. Embrace opportunities to learn as often as you invite chances to teach, even more than. Observe and internalize the lessons surrounding you daily. Utilize everything God gave you. Your goal is to leave this world fulfilled, yet empty.

Let us pray.

i am INTELLIGENT

Father, thank You for waking me in my right mind.

God, thank You for my natural intellect, my common sense, and that which I have acquired through professional study and life experiences. Thank You for exposing me to different ideals, insights, locations, and cultures. Thank You for creating similarities and differences in others, and reminding me not to ridicule, critique or destroy them based upon my level of comprehension of their significance. Thank You for positioning me to learn, adapt, grow, and evolve. It is my desire to please You, to serve You in a way that brings honor to Your kingdom and light into the dark places of this world. Father, forgive me for not always walking in the fullness of who You created me to be. Don't let me jeopardize my focus or abandon my goals. Don't allow my intellect to outsmart, override, or discredit my discernment. Teach me not to overthink or analyze to a fault. Channel my meticulous nature into productivity and efficiency that will bring glory to You and increase in my career or ares of professional expertise. Anoint my speech that I may clearly and succinctly communicate my thoughts according to Your wishes and desires. Anoint my ears to listen and to hear the ideas of others with an open heart and open mind. Coat my tone in Your compassion and Your patience that I never come across condescending or insulting, even when I oppose the opinions and perspectives being expressed by the other party. Teach me how to lead all of my conversations and interactions with love. Remind me not to deflect, but to always make time for interrogative conversations that yield clarity and dismiss ignorance. Allow my thoughts to begin and end with you in mind, to be filtered by your grace, and to consistently lack assumptions and judgment. Because of You, i am intelligent.

In Jesus' name, Amen.

Get out of your way.

You are blocking your own progress for all of the wrong reasons. You are separating your identity from that of the Creator and it's causing you to become weak, pessimistic, and weary. You stopped believing you could. You stopped imagining the possibilities   You ceased to seek after new opportunities. You failed to expand your horizons. You've doubted yourself for far too long.

The questions are: When was that seed of discouragement first planted? Why did you let it grow? Who benefits from you being small? How does shrinking yourself serve a true purpose? What are you going to do to change it?

The answers are easily defined, but not as easily implemented. In order for the depth of your power to be exposed, you have to have some hard conversations with yourself. You have to decide to change, consistently. You have to make yourself a priority. You have to choose Him and allow Him to show you why choosing you is a necessity. You can't fight when you're malnourished. (Well, you can, but you will likely lose or severely injure yourself in the process, so don't try.) You can't win the battle (or the war) when you won't do the work of self-discovery and evaluation. It's not to say that you won't have weaknesses. It is to say that you must submit those to God and allow His strength to be perfected in their midst. That exchange is a win-win situation, but in order to mount the championship stage of this race, you have to fortify yourself, firmly, in the power He gave you.

Get out of your way. Start now.

Let us pray.

CONFESSION X

i am POWERFUL

Father, thank You for my emotional & spiritual resilience.

My internal compass is guided by Your spirit. It is from Your reservoir of protection that I draw my security. With You, I dwell in a sacred place. With You, I am infused with confidence and vigor, dominion and authority. Even in my fragility, You are there, perfecting the fortitude You've placed within me. Thank You for stability and reassurance. Thank You for direction and protection. Thank You for thinking enough of me to create an eternal connection within me that ensures I am never without You. Thank You for positioning me to win in the toughest of circumstances, that even when I perceive loss and failure, You are there to remind me of the lessons and the triumphs that would not otherwise exist had I not persevered. Father, forgive me for not always walking in the fullness of who You created me to be. Teach me how to embrace the totality of who I am, authentically, boldly, confidently, and unapologetically, not quietly or ashamed, but freely and lovingly. Remind me that I was created in Your image and that I am indeed the product of Your desires, a precise and perfected vision translated into tangible form. Disconnect me from those who are intimidated by Your glory and seek to dishonor it, You, or me. If I must remain affiliated with dishonorable people, grant me the patience with them that You have with me. Allow me to positively influence them to change their ways, rather than be lured into unhealthy habits, mindsets, and behaviors based upon our interactions. Never permit me to doubt my ability to stand in my truth and to conquer the impossible. Because of You, i am powerful.

In Jesus' name, Amen.

Before you make this confession, go and take look at yourself in the mirror. I'll wait....

Welcome back.

Pause. Did you do it for real? If you did, thank you. If you didn't ... *insert sigh here* You're holding up progress. Look now. Please. (Don't be hard-headed for no reason.) Do it now.... Thank you.

Play. Now, what did you see? Did you marvel at the shape of your eyes and lips? Were you enamored by your skin tone? Did you revel at the body and texture of your hair or the lack thereof? Did your appearance bring a smile to your face? Or, were you "underwhelmed"? Did you immediately focus in on the blemishes on your cheeks? Were you suddenly reminded that you're overdue for an eyebrow wax? Did your reflection bring you pleasure or pain? Excitement or guilt? Seriously, what did you see?

More often than not, we see our defects and deficiencies long before we focus on our attributes and assets. We view ourselves through the guise of public opinion rather than from the vantage point of the Almighty God. We shape our standards of beauty around popularity, viral posts, media images, and highlight reels, diluting our taste and appreciation for ourselves with every view. The problem with this audacious approach is that its indicative of an assumed flaw at the hands of God. Somehow, He got the calculations wrong when he decided our height, weight, and what features should comprise and adorn our bodies. Rejecting the physical attributes God gave us naturally not only shows a lack of cognizance of and gratitude for His artistry, but it also paralyzes us or diminishes how we show up in the world. God deserves better than that, and so do you.

Let us pray.

i am BEAUTIFUL

Father, thank You for my physical attributes and mental stoicism.

Thank You for teaching me the two go hand in hand to establish my unique beauty. Thank You for not allowing me to take any feature for granted, but to be constantly reminded to value Your original and remarkable creation as it is. Thank You for my temperament, my personality, my intellect, my ambitions, my poise, and my spirit. Thank You for crafting me, molding me, and shaping me in the exact fashion that You did. Father, forgive me for not always walking in the fullness of who You created me to be. We are constantly exposed to various degrees, measurements, and definitions of beauty that were not established by You. Teach me how to ignore them and look to You for affirmation, validation, confirmation, and exaltation. Don't allow me to be crushed by the limited perceptions and jaded perspectives of my peers, coworkers, family members, friends, or miscellaneous members of society. Allow me to evaluate myself positively so that deformities and imperfections don't disturb me to the point of shame or hiding, but rather, root me in humility and appreciation for what I have. I never want to surmise my worth or another's value solely based upon what I see. When I am tempted to do so, correct me. In the areas where I seek improvement or enhancement, give me the devotion to see it through. Guide me in a healthy way to accomplish the goal, one that doesn't disrupt my evolution, belittle my process, disregard my identity, or disrespect my state of being at any point along the journey. Teach me not to compare, but to embrace all of me: the good, the bad, the ugly, and the indifferent, fully recognizing that You already do, and anyone who is truly for me, undoubtedly, will too. Because of You, i am beautiful.

In Jesus' name, Amen.

There is a divine essence in being a woman. We possess unexplainable qualities that leave some in awe and render others speechless. Many marvel at our strength, tenacity, and perseverance. Others are hypnotized by our wit, charm, and personalities. Our innate propensity for self-discovery and introspection commands self-awareness and confidence, which is admittedly attractive.

While there is nothing wrong with celebrating our beauty, we are often ostracized or chastised if we lean too far in that direction. It's like there exists an imaginary line that we dare not cross, especially as women who love God, else, there is trouble in the city. Attire is over-analyzed. Reputations are scrutinized. Character is criticized. The contradictions and double standards experienced, particularly in comparison to our male counterparts, can be demeaning, disheartening, and even intimidating.

The freedom in embracing all of you is that you are no longer subjected to, bound by, or suffering from the whim of people's opinions. The parts of you that make others uncomfortable are no longer your responsibility. Your physical features aren't determinates of your worth and your body can't be exchanged for acceptance.

On the flip side, you must remember to whom much is given, much is required. God didn't grant you the favor of beauty for you to pervert it and distort it for personal gain. Your body is a temple and should be treated as such. Sex is an exquisite gift you should share in a covenant relationship. It is not a coping mechanism to overcome insecurities, a weapon in your arsenal to manipulate outcomes, or a temptation you must give in to each time it calls. One of the sacred parts of your femininity is mastering how and knowing when to harness your sexuality and finesse your sensuality.

Let us pray.

CONFESSION XII

i am SENSUAL & SEXUAL

Father, thank You for my femininity.

Thank You for my features, those I love and those I pray will evolve. Thank You for allowing me to feel and express emotion. Thank You for creating affection and physical touch that can permeate my soul in the best and worst of times. Thank You for seeing me as a person, not as an object, and for giving me the option to choose with whom I share the most intimate parts of me. Thank You for giving me purpose that equally relies upon my intellect, spiritual fortitude, and emotional intelligence, as much as it does my body. Thank You for teaching me the difference between sexuality and intimacy, lascivious behavior and mere flirtation. Thank You for permission to discover my likes and desires without condemnation. Thank You for not restricting me to the "norms" that misinformed and uneducated portions of society, the church, or religion may attempt to dictate. Thank You for defining my role(s) based upon You, not my partner, my physical attributes, or the lack thereof. Father, forgive me for not always walking in the fullness of who You created me to be. I want to please You in every way. I want to represent You with class, style, dignity, and grace. I want to be free to accentuate what You gave me without having to worry about compromising my call or my ability to effectively witness to Your people. Don't allow me to be reduced to the ideas of pleasure I can provide a man. Teach me to reject stereotypes, not to succumb to them, accommodate them, or try and circumvent them. Obliterate the scars, residue, and effects of past trauma where I was disrespected, taken advantage of, assaulted, or violated. Don't allow any negative circumstances and illegitimate quests for power to rob me of the liberation You bestowed upon me. Because of You, i am sensual & sexual.

In Jesus' name, Amen.

Evolving into womanhood is challenging, to say the least. Balancing personal desires, ambitions, illnesses, hormones, careers, etc, is like an ongoing juggling match with new balls being thrown into the mix on a daily or even hourly basis. As we grow and mature, we are often reminded of the lessons taught to us by our parents and caregivers. We find ourselves saying things they've said or doing things they've done, heeding their instructions and yielding the benefits of their wisdom. Suddenly, almost magically, they start to make a ridiculous amount of sense and you're filled with immense gratitude that they didn't randomly pack your things and ship you off to Oz or Zamunda when you were younger :).

Ironically, life has a way of making everything come full circle. As much as you adore those who shaped your development, and may love to reflect on the memories, it's easy to overwhelm yourself with pressures to make them proud. You want to represent them well, so you embark on a path they would deem pleasing and acceptable. Now, if that path is the same one you would choose for yourself, you are winning. Proceed. However, if you are living their dream and not yours, you have to release yourself from the burden of their expectations. Killing parts of you in order to appease parts of them is not healthy. It can lead to bitterness, resentment, anger, and frustration that come seeping out at the most inopportune moments.

Do yourself (and them) a favor. Stop chasing their vision and reach towards His. Do it unashamed, without remorse or regret. Share your truth with them and live your best life. Even if they don't agree, they will still love you. Ultimately, their goals (for you) were simply their way of securing your future, making sure you would thrive and prosper. If you manage to get "there" by taking a different route, it won't even matter.

Let us pray.

i am A DAUGHTER

Father, thank You for my parents and those who raised me.

Thank You for choosing them to birth Your creation. Thank You for blessing their union with my existence, for an opportunity to become a testament of Your divinity and omnipotence. Thank You for their vision for my life, for their guidance, for their protection, for their wisdom, their encouragement, their patience, their forgiveness, their compassion, and most certainly, for their love. Thank You for the example they set with lifestyles that are dedicated to You, or at least giving me the freedom to explore what that looked like. Thank You for giving them a heart of service, a desire to leave this world and every environment they encounter better than it was before their arrival. Thank You for creating a bond between them that no man can break and a stable, nurturing household to support my growth and evolution. If there were inconsistencies in my environment, thank You for not inhibiting my development or aborting my assignment, as a result. Father, forgive me for not always walking in the fullness of who You created me to be. Allow my life to be representative of the seeds sowed into me or despite them. Grant me favor to be able to care and provide for my parents or guardians until their last days, that they never lack anything. Keep them healthy, safe, and protected. Honor their obedience to You with long life, filled with joy and abundance. Teach me how to properly communicate their worth in ways that honor their personalities and love languages. Remind me to keep them before You in prayer and to always check in to make sure they are okay. Position me to win in life so they know their efforts, and the sacrifices made on my behalf, were not in vain. As I strive to please You, allow them to benefit greatly from each of my endeavors. Because of You, i am a daughter.

In Jesus' name, Amen.

They are your best friends and your biggest antagonizers. They can torture you like no one in the world, but wouldn't dare let anyone else get close enough to try. During school-age years, they are your allies, particularly when joining forces against your parents, babysitters, or adults in general, but they can also be the troublemakers who cause you to reap a punishment you didn't even earn. They are your sisters. They share some of your deepest secrets and offer laughter, wisdom, and encouragement through some of the darkest times in your life. If you're truly blessed, they later bestow upon you the honor of being an aunt to awesome nieces and nephews that you can spoil extravagantly. You take great pride in creating memorable experiences for them because they are amazing little replicas of their mother, but also because you know, when the indulgence ends, you get to send them back home, without apology or contrition :).

Having a sister is an irrefutable joy that cannot be compared to any other relationship, not even that of having a brother. Yet, there are times when you live in their shadows. You wonder if you will measure up to their accomplishments, or if somehow, you will be tripped up by their mistakes. You question if their results, or an absence of, will be yours. You set your boundaries, parameters, and limitations based upon what they did or did not do. That is where the trouble sets in, and that is what you must commit to stop doing.

Your sister is not your competition. She is not a liability or an enemy. She is a reflection of God's love for you, a cheerleader, protector, and shining beacon of light. You don't have to be like her unless you want to be. She's not expecting you to, and neither should you. She's waiting for you to step into greatness so she can brag about your awesomeness. Give her an abundance of reasons to boast. Lay it on thick! She wants to see you win.

Let us pray.

i am A SISTER

Father, thank You for my siblings and friends that feel like family.

Thank You for extending examples of support, for creating role models, and for allowing me to be one for others. Thank You for the laughs, the lessons, and the love that comes from these types of connections. These people understand me, in a way that others don't, without great deals of explanation or long stints of exploration. They just get me. That, in and of itself, is a form of validation of my existence and verification of my purpose that I didn't know I needed until it was received. Thank You for their sincerity, their energy, their peace, and their vibes. I appreciate the balance they bring to my life. They are crazy, yet practical, silly, but intellectual, fiery, yet comforting. Their loyalty comes from an irreplaceable, authentic place of sincerity that I attribute only to You. Father, forgive me for not always walking in the fullness of who You created me to be. As we continue to grow and experience various facets of life, don't allow us to forget who You have called us to be, as individuals or to one another, or to take advantage of this precious bond You've established between us. Remind us to reach out to one another, to continue to be there to serve the relationship however needed. Teach me to support even when tough love is warranted. Allow me to remain open to their perspective, especially when it's opposite of mine. Undergird our communication with truth, so that we can always depend on one another for earnest development. Don't allow me to miss opportunities to celebrate their victories and be their one-woman marketing and advertising agency. Let me always honor the "treat others as you want to be treated" notion, but never forget to treat them as they desire to be treated, just the same. Because of You, i am a sister.

In Jesus' name, Amen.

You dreamed about the day you would add three letters to the front of your name. You pontificated regarding what your new initials would be or if they would even change. "To hyphenate or not to hyphenate," may have become the question. You planned out the wedding ceremony, selected the perfect dress and location, fantasized about your ring, and may have even finalized the menu for the reception long before you even had a prospect for marriage.

Or, maybe you didn't. You may be one who isn't intrinsically swoon by the concept of uniting with one individual for a lifetime. It wasn't something you contemplated or ever considered. Then, you met "him". He was cool. You liked the vibe and then, "it" just kind of... happened.

In either case, and the myriad of scenarios that exist in between extremes, you became the covenant partner to a man. Hopefully, he is one who loves and adores you, one who follows after the examples of Christ and the church, as well as great men that came before him, one who shares with you, not just his heart, but his life, his dreams, his challenges, his fears, and his aspirations. He communicates his ups and downs, and invites you into his space for you to help him build. You two are partners. It's a testament to the power of love, patience, forgiveness, and commitment.

All of that is to be treasured. Your marriage is to be defended and protected at all costs. You have a responsibility to God, yourself, and your husband to show up, daily, as the woman God fashioned in His image, not one who hides her desires, coddles her wisdom, or undermines her destiny out of fear of rejection. Your marriage deserves a whole man and a whole woman. Don't succumb to only sharing pieces of you. Don't be so impressed by your title that you neglect the woman who gave it to you.

Let us pray.

i am A WIFE

Father, thank You for my friend, my lover, my spouse.

Thank You for choosing him to cover me, to love me, to protect me, to walk with me through life. Thank You for the mutual respect we share, for the sacred covenant we honor, and for the legacy we work together to build. Thank You for blessing me with someone after Your heart, who consistently seeks to please You. Thank You for teaching me how to submit to the vision You've crafted for our lives together and the order of our household that works best for us. Father, forgive me for not always walking in the fullness of who You created me to be. As we attempt to work together to design a union that is not only acceptable to You, but also fulfilling to us, and attractive to those who don't know You, keep us humble. Remove any judgment or condemnation from our language and thought patterns. Teach me how to love him, how to be in us, without losing me, and most importantly, without losing You. Show me how to maintain proper identity, individuality, and independence, all while prioritizing my assignment to him, according to Your will. Allow me to master communicating and expressions of his love language(s), as he works to do the same for me. Teach us to laugh, to heal, to blend planning with spontaneity, to enjoy our union in every way. Remind me to affirm him as he is, while encouraging him to become all You have purposed, to always provide a safe place of rest, refuge, and solace he can depend upon when he's feeling weak, inferior, or enraged by the outside world. Don't allow me to take him or us for granted. Teach me how to intercede when he won't communicate or doesn't know how. Remind us never to look outside of our relationship for anything we need to sustain it. Prepare me to grow with him, as I evolve in You. Because of You, i am a wife.

In Jesus' name, Amen.

There is no feeling like the one you experience when a child sees you enter the room and they take off in your direction. Watching their eyes twinkle in excitement and their faces light up in appreciation for your presence is one of life's undeniable fortunes. Their unconditional love and exuberance is irreplaceable. The ability to bring a child into the world or to serve as a safe haven for them is one of a woman's most honorable, sacred, precious, and revered gifts. While a child's embrace can give you the motivation you need to push through the toughest of times, the continual responsibility of maintaining their health, safety, and well-being can sometimes be overwhelming.

Many women are guilty of losing themselves in the lives and lifestyles of their children. You're focused on managing your household while coordinating their schedules, cultivating their gifts while challenging their insecurities. Meanwhile, back at the ranch, you're still navigating your own faith, career, fantasies, and evolution, all while attempting to maintain a healthy, respectable relationship with your husband or your child's father, if you're no longer together. It. Is. A. Lot.

God doesn't require you to cease being a woman once you become a mother. You don't have to negate every other part of yourself for the sake of your child. Any mother would do anything to ensure their child stays out of harm's way, but don't use your children as an excuse or justification for giving up on yourself. As miraculous as being a mother is, if God called you to do more, embrace it and work towards it. Alternatively, if their care is your sole responsibility, don't degrade or diminish that. Teach your children about priorities, prayer, flexibility, and wellness. Show your boys and girls you can have it ALL. Maybe not at the same time, but it's definitely within reach when you commit to getting it. Be their proof.

Let us pray.

i am A MOTHER

Father, thank You for my children, my legacy.

Thank You for those I birthed naturally, those I adopted, and those who chose me to serve them in this capacity. Thank You for the opportunity to create life and impart wisdom into their existence. Thank You for trusting me with their intellect, their faith, their personality, their value system, their courage, their independence, their self worth, and their dependence on You. Thank You for giving me the strength and courage needed to support the king and queen in them. Thank You for showing me and their father a healthy pattern of communication and interaction to properly shape their understanding of relationships. Father, forgive me for not always walking in the fullness of who You created me to be. My children may not always make the decisions I suggest or those I would desire and approve. Don't allow that to hinder our relationship or prohibit me from supporting them. Grant me patience and relatability to understand their situation(s) from their point of view. Surround us with people who can tap into their gifts and talents, and assist me in ensuring they are properly channeled, managed, and produced for Your glory. Don't ever allow them to question my desire to be a part of their lives. Strengthen my maternal instincts and my spiritual discernment, so I will know when they need me or someone for reassurance, direction, affirmation, laughter, reprieve, and peace. Give me the tools to craft love, character, integrity, responsibility, passion, compassion, and confidence into the foundational crevices of their souls. Show me how to embed into their beings that there is no place like home, that they are always welcome and safe in my arms, and while no one will love them as I do, that others' love is a venerated privilege to behold. Because of You, i am a mother.

In Jesus' name, Amen.

Your friends are the family members you get to choose. You have some that share common interests and others who serve as the voice of reason during times of uncertainty. The best ones offer smiles and laughs in exchange for tears and frustration. They bring out the best in you. They see beyond the current circumstance or situation, and they welcome your evolution. They walk beside you, endorse you, subsidize your endeavors, love you, and offer depth to your life experiences. As much as they bring into your life, you add to theirs. That's the beauty of reciprocal relationships. They are not one-sided, but mutually beneficial and fulfilling.

With an army of supporters in your squad or on your team, it's easy to become "one of the crew". While it's amazing for the camaraderie and fellowship, it can be detrimental to your personal development IF you don't continue to work on yourself for the duration of those relationships. If you find yourself jealous of your bestie's latest victory or caught in the comparison trap between your accomplishments and those of others, chances are, you are punishing yourself for the untapped potential that lies within you. You're not a bad friend or an inherently evil person. You're bound by your circumstances or self-limiting beliefs and embittered to see someone actually doing the things you've only dreamed about.

Your life is not over. Time has not run out. You simply have to commit to doing something different. Lean into gifts that are currently lying dormant. Take the class. Start dating again. Change jobs. Move. Do what you need to do to create a life you don't have to vacation from.

The best friends accept you as you are and champion you while you're becoming all you desire to be. Make sure you are your friend first, before you expect someone else to be, and so your standards are set appropriately.

Let us pray.

CONFESSION XVII

i am A FRIEND

Father, thank You for the blessing of meaningful, healthy, and insightful engagement with others.

Thank You for birthing my community, so that I have people to travel with during the ebbs and flows of my journey with You and in You. Thank You for modeling true friendship in Your word, so that I might have a standard to aspire to and uphold. Thank You for the confidants and the secure bonds that allow me to reveal all of me without embarrassment or condemnation. Thank You for the joy, the hysterics, the peace, and the fulfillment that comes along with genuine connection. Father, forgive me for not always walking in the fullness of who You created me to be. I ask You to purge me of anything that is not like You, anything that could hinder me from building and sustaining long lasting, reciprocal, wholesome relationships. Show me the parts of me that need to be healed, so that I don't project my insecurities and idiosyncrasies on those who are attempting to be an example of Your love towards me. Teach me how to hear their quiet whispers for help, assistance, guidance and reassurance, as boldly and distinctly as I relish in their loud screams of ambition, satisfaction, and enjoyment. Don't allow me to ever become so self-involved that I ignore the needs and wants of those around me. Remind me that it is not my job to save them, but to introduce them to You so that You can. Prevent me from falling into destructive habits, condoning detrimental behavior, or disguising my disappointments for the sake of their comfort. Grant me patience. Keep me grounded in You, never attempting to replace our relationship with any person in this world. Remain as my Savior, so that I can serve as a companion, counselor, and support to and for others. Because of You, i am a friend.

In Jesus' name, Amen.

You're confident in your skills, talents, and abilities. You're a boss in your business and career. You have healthy relationships. You take care of yourself. You look fabulous. You consistently attempt to outperform your last goal and achievement and push the boundaries of who you are. You worked to heal from and overcome your past and mistakes. You're amazing and you've done amazing things. You should be proud, but is there more? You're engineering your to-do list, but what about His?

How many times have you been in a meeting and noticed something about a coworker or team member, a trait, characteristic or emotion, to which, everyone else seemed oblivious? When was the last time you heard about a situation and literally empathized to the degree that you physically felt someone's pain, anguish, fear, or disappointment in your body? You woke up last night, from the same dream, for the fifth night in a row. Did you write it down? Do you know what it means?

The thing is, you may have conquered every obvious mountain that has stood in your way along your journey, particularly in the eyes of man, but what about in the eyes of God? How confident and competent are you in the profundity and legitimacy of your relationship with Him? Have you considered that those private battles you fight, particularly on behalf of others, may be because you have the gift of intercession? Imagine how much stronger you would be if you released yourself from the definition and identity you've previously associated with the term "intercessor"and accepted that it is a part of you that you haven't nurtured, developed, or completely tapped into? It may not be your only gift or even a dominant one, but be intentional about evaluating your prayer life, talking to God consistently and with an open spirit, to ensure you aren't ignoring Him, His call, His voice, or a part of your assignment.

Let us pray.

CONFESSION XVIII

i am AN INTERCESSOR

Father, thank You for Your Holy Spirit.

Thank You for discernment to know when You are speaking, when You are leading, and when You are directing me to say or to do. Thank You for sweet communion with You, for being close enough to You that I can always hear Your voice. Thank You for teaching me how to trust You in the dark places, leaning on You to be my eternal light. Father, forgive me for not always walking in the fullness of who You created me to be. As You have commissioned me to stand in the gap for others, teach me how to obey Your will without taking on others burdens as my own. Show me how to carry the weights You've ordained for me and to leave all others in Your presence, at Your feet. Keep my environment clear of chaos, clutter, and confusion, so that I never miss Your instructions. When I am busy or drifting into a space that would render me powerless and conformed to a circumstance or a persona You didn't create for me, pull me back, so that my prayers remain effective. When You need me to draw nearer, teach me how to fast and consecrate, praying with more intensity and fervor, so I can impact Your people and Your kingdom. Grant me courage for this assignment. Comfort me when I am lonely. Don't allow my frustrations or the isolation of my assignment cause me to abort the calling. When I don't have the words to say, like You did for Simon (Peter), say a prayer for me. Intercede on my behalf, so that no stone is left unturned, no problem is left uncovered, and no resolution is left undiscovered. Rebuke the Savior Complex from dwelling inside of me. Don't allow my energy to be thwarted or usurped by things and people that don't concern me. Prevent me from manipulating or pimping my gift, using it as a means to an end, rather than as a tool to help mend. Because of You, i am an intercessor.

In Jesus' name, Amen.

It is better to give than to receive. The joy gained from moments of authentic service can't be compared to any other form of fulfillment. It reminds you of the power of love. It underscores a spirit of gratitude. It reveals selflessness and even surrender to a purpose beyond simply existing. It honors God, His principles, and His heart.

While enjoying the benefits of an assignment to serve, it is quite easy to pervert its intention or inappropriately process a moment of sacrifice and planting through an unhealthy need for validation or attention. It is also common for servants to use their gifts as coping mechanisms to avoid dealing with other issues that may be prevalent in their lives at a particular time.

Don't let that be you. Ditch the ulterior motives when serving. Do it from a sincere heart or don't do it at all. Further, don't use your work and efforts towards others as a justification for not completing the personal assignments God has entrusted to you. He knows when you're hiding from Him. He can see the guilt in your commitments. His deity transcends your intellect. Don't shy away from the talent and aptitude He's placed inside of you. Trust Him to show you how your service can glorify Him. Allow Him to unlock the doors of your heart, to heal you from any brokenness, so that pure bliss is what resonates from your acts of kindness and contagious generosity.

Shouldering your deliverance and seizing your liberty will encourage and inspire others to do the same. Serve with gladness, with boldness, with confidence, with zest, with zeal, with passion, and with excellence. Serve as a whole and complete vessel, one who is blessed with wisdom and discernment, open to share the genuineness of her oblations with others.

Let us pray.

CONFESSION XIX

i am A SERVANT

Father, thank You for teaching me how to serve.

Thank You for Your humility. Thank You for how You fashioned ministry as a selfless act. Thank You for being the ultimate sacrifice and supporting me in my own expedition and voyage of discovery in how to give the best of me to others without losing or belittling myself in the process. Thank You for leading with love. Thank You for thinking enough of me to grant me the opportunity to carry out Your great commission, to help people, to bless people, to assist people in accomplishing their goals, and to support them, genuinely, in whatever manner they deem most beneficial. Father, forgive me for not always walking in the fullness of who You created me to be. As I strive to live a life of positive impact, influence, and inspiration, keep my motives and intentions pure. Don't allow me to serve out of obligation or requirement, but more so, out of the abundance of my heart and my earnest objective to push people towards their potential. Don't let my service be misinterpreted or misguided. Don't allow me to use my service to disguise a need for validation or affirmation from people. You affirm me. You validate me. Show me how to maintain a befitting vantage point. Give me a clean heart. Endow me with the power of Your Holy Spirit. Grant me the wisdom and courage to accept only the invitations (to serve) that will invoke Your presence, and to decline or redirect all others that could jeopardize or compromise my reputation in You. Let the words of my mouth and the meditations of my heart always be acceptable to You. Let my service be a flare of radiant and engaging light that shines brightly on my trek, and ultimately directs others to You. Scale my service in accordance with the value I can provide. I want to be ready to do what you need, whenever You need me to do it. Because of You, i am a servant.

In Jesus' name, Amen.

Everyday is an opportunity to build, to grow, to evolve, to learn. Situations and circumstances open our eyes to different perspectives that assist us in navigating new terrain. "That's the way we've always done it," is seemingly touted from a place of strength, courage, and power. Yet, it is often a facade; one that covers a debilitating fear of the unknown, a predictable doubt regarding the unfamiliar, and an inability to submit to the impetus change can evoke and the ingenuity it can offer.

We are all commissioned to embrace the newness of each day that unfolds, awakening our thoughts and availing ourselves to discover more about who we are and those we are traveling along this journey to impact. It is in our best interest to increase our capacity for not only the things that make us comfortable, but most importantly those that challenge us and propel us forward.

Recognizing and appreciating the difficulties that surround us will build our perseverance. We need not shrink back and pull away from the hard lessons life exposes. We must push past the insecurities to enrich our personal development. God wants you to know more about your family, your friends, your career, your purpose, your character, and things of that nature, but more than anything, He wants you to know Him and to know yourself. Doing so requires a few trips around the sun and a relentless spirit that won't let go until it learns a thing or two.

Commit yourself to experience all that life has to offer. Resist the temptation to be limited by what has never been, but rather be unwavering in your determination to expose it, traverse it, and conquer it. As you learn more about others, you not only help yourself, but you also position your heart to remain filled with understanding, love, and compassion.

Let us pray.

i am A STUDENT

Father, thank You for the ability to absorb knowledge, to grasp concepts, and to process information.

I'm grateful to be a product of Your thoughts. I'm honored to be a vessel that is open to comprehend, to develop, and to mature. Thank You for Your character, for Your nature, for peaking my interest and welcoming me to embrace my curiosity. Thank You for allowing me to see obstacles as opportunities to establish or reaffirm myself as a victor, not a victim. Thank You for eliminating excuses and barriers that would otherwise aim to block me from gaining experience, increasing my value, and welcoming the lessons You are teaching me. Father, forgive me for not always walking in the fullness of who You created me to be. Train my eyes to see the possibility and potential in all situations so that I'm never limited by my previous exposure or restricted to my prior experiences. Reinforce my propensity to always dig deeper for revelation, so that I might substantiate my claims in Your truth and corroborate my facts with Your will. Reveal to me the spaces where people have something that I need or that You want me to have. Craft my imagination in such a way that I explore in my dreams and wake up feeling empowered to implement those ideas. Don't ever quench my thirst for knowledge. Don't ever kill my interrogative nature. Don't allow negative moments in my past to overshadow the path to my future. Don't allow me to become content or comfortable with where I am when You have so much more to offer. Keep me open. Keep me available. Keep me positioned. Keep me stable. Keep me pliable. Keep me humble. Keep me in pursuit of any and everything You have purposed for me. Keep me postured to learn. Keep me forever in Your care. Because of You, i am a student.

In Jesus' name, Amen.

Maya Angelou said, "When you learn, teach. When you get, give." The principles are simple. Part of the purpose of your acquisition of anything is what you are able to do with it, and how you can share it to positively transform the world around you. Your knowledge is no exception to the rule. You have a voice that is strong because it overcame adversity, one that is powerful because it was fortified through false accusations and ridicule. Your voice, your truth, your experiences have worth and value. They are irreplaceable assets that speak to the core of your being, the diversity of your perspective, and the heritage of your legacy. You were put here to impart, to empower, to propel, to enrich, and to inspire. You matter.

When we lose, particularly in situations where winning seemed inevitable or almost guaranteed, we often internalize the entire situation as a failure. We process the disappointment from a place so deep that we have to borderline deploy the National Guard to come to our rescue. It is in these moments of brokenness that we are often tormented and teased by the enemy. His negative thoughts began to consume you, leaving you in a silent battle of anguish. Sometimes, instead of shutting him down, redirecting our attention or declaring victory over ourselves, we crumble under the pressure. We begin to believe his lies, we become the victim, and we shirk back into representatives of ourselves, as opposed to standing in the authority of the cross and walking as a conqueror.

Today, remember that no situation is greater than the God you serve. Regardless of how tough it may seem or how hard you may have fallen, you can get back up. You can learn from everything that transpired. You can overcome by the word of your testimony. You can always teach somebody something.

Let us pray.

CONFESSION XXI

i am AN EDUCATOR

Father, thank You for granting me the ability to empower others through education.

Thank You for teaching me that I don't have to be employed by a school or in a classroom to offer truth, wisdom, inspiration, or value. Thank You for positioning me to influence those around me, so they can emulate the lessons and behaviors in future circumstances. Thank You for giving me knowledge and insight, which can compel someone to look to You for guidance, direction, and assistance. Thank You for gracing me with courage to endure the hard times and tribulations, knowing they would offer me a stronger vantage point, renewed compassion, and a well-rounded and exquisitely vetted point of view. Thank You for instructing me in conflict resolution and edifying me regarding diplomacy, so I may consistently practice listening to both sides of an argument before formulating my opinion. Father, forgive me for not always walking in the fullness of who You created me to be. God, continue to school me, guide me, and prepare me. Don't allow my abilities to be capped off or limited based upon what I know in this moment. Position me in rooms where I am not the smartest person. Engulf me in environments that force me to "level up" and enhance my dexterity, my artistry, my creativity, my versatility, and my aptitude. Authenticate my sphere of influence and my network, so that I can funnel what I've learned to those who desire more and certainly those who need it most. Give me excellent communication skills and a clear and concise message to reach my intended audience, removing all barriers, and resulting in life changing, transformative experiences for each person I am graced to cultivate and inculcate a sense of determination and responsibility. Because of You, i am an educator.

In Jesus' name, Amen.

Do you remember being a child, maybe in elementary school, and at some point being asked, "What do you want to be when you grow up?" Do you recall how excited you were to profess your destined career path? An astronaut or a pilot. A chef or a surgeon. A lawyer or a movie star. The possibilities were endless. At some point, you may have even imagined yourself in your future office or on the big screen. You were so audacious that you weren't just going to be a nurse, but you were going to coach in the NBA at the same time. You dreamed and you dreamed BIG! You imagined the car you would drive and the house you would live in. You thought about how you would shower friends and family with gifts and expressions of love, sponsoring community activities, taking long, extravagant vacations, but always being excited to return to this amazing life you'd built for yourself.

What happened to those dreams? How many of them have you fulfilled? If none or for the remainder, what exactly are you waiting on? What made you give up on ... you?

Whatever career path you've chosen, are you excelling or just settling for whatever you've been offered? Have you convinced yourself that you're too old, or under qualified, or weak, or broke, or broken? That it's too late to be the you of your childhood wishes? If you have, allow me to introduce one last question for your consideration. Could you be wrong?

Believe you are more than a conqueror. Set aside some time to strategize and then execute. Build the business while you work for someone else. Take the class during your lunch break or after hours. Study your craft instead of catching up on the latest news and entertainment. Make your dream come true. Give yourself permission to become. You are a boss!

Let us pray.

CONFESSION XXII

i am A PROFESSIONAL

Father, thank You for an occupation that offers provision and latitude.

Thank You for my strengths, my weaknesses, my opportunities, and for unveiling the threats that could hinder my productivity and my profitability. Thank You for allowing me to network with like-minded people who have similar agendas and goals. Thank You for teaching me to embrace the challenges of my field, so that I can continue to develop into a greater version of myself. Thank You for the courage to boldly step into new spaces with expertise and capabilities that will be recognized and appreciated. Thank You for allowing my gifts to make room for me. Thank You for permitting me access to earn a livable wage and not to be intimidated by new environments that will expand my reach and enlarge my territory. Father, forgive me for not always walking in the fullness of who You created me to be. I ask that You would lead me as I attempt to establish myself and advance in my career. Teach me when to stay, when to move, and where to go. Remind me that all money isn't good money and that every door opened is not one that should be entered. Give me the tools needed to succeed and the compassion to lead in a manner that compels others to follow me. Redirect me away from companies that uphold a culture that doesn't align with my personal values. Plant me in organizations that wholeheartedly accept all of me and position me to thrive, not solely as an employee, but as a human being. Show me how to remain viable, flexible, and ambitious. Don't force me to choose between my career and my family, but furnish me with the courage, insight, and divine prioritization to nourish and maintain them in a manner which is enjoyable to us and pleasing to You. Because of You, i am a professional.

In Jesus' name, Amen.

Working for someone is admirable. It is the gateway to erudition, culture, and training in a professional environment. Taking what you know and channeling it, focusing it, and packaging it into a product or service that can benefit others is a game changer. Successfully owning your own business offers freedom and flexibility, along with pride and a legacy that will extend far beyond your mortal existence. To take nothing and turn it into something is one of our most cherished capabilities as humans. It is when you transcend from a creation to a creator. The ability to exhibit all that's necessary to create offers an indescribable sensation of emotions ranging from jubilee to accomplishment to trepidation and later, relief.

It is a common practice to evaluate your status in life in comparison to another's success. Doing so will often leave you disturbed and disgruntled, feeling like you took a wrong turn at some point. The problem in this behavior is that it is immeasurably, irrefutably, and fundamentally flawed in its nature. Your triumphs, victories, and accolades can't be predicated upon or validated by those of someone else. Comparisons should be reserved for analyzing who you are in reference to who God has called you to be, nothing more or less.

Don't diminish the traits He crafted inside of you. Stop self-rejecting. That business concept may not be as crazy as you think or even if it is, maybe it is supposed to be. We won't ever know if you don't take the time and put in the effort to bring it to fruition. Currently, it's "just" an idea, but what if you did it? What if your product is what the world is in desperate need of? What if your service alters an entire industry? If you're scared, do it anyway! Don't feed into your fears or allow them to cripple you out of productivity. File the paperwork. Establish the business. Open the business banking account, and get this show on the road!

Let us pray.

CONFESSION XXIII

i am AN ENTREPRENEUR

Father, thank You for giving me a vision to manifest in the Earth.

Thank You for planting a seed inside of me and giving me the work ethic to plant it, water it, prune it, and watch it grow. Thank You for the joy that comes along with witnessing the idea come to life. Thank You for the personal fulfillment I am granted each time a client receives my product or service. Thank You for teaching me how to fine tune my offerings and present them in a palatable format for my target market. Thank you for keeping me honest, integral, and focused on being their solution or fulfilling their desire. Thank you for teaching me how to solve problems, strategize, save, budget, organize, hire, fire, sympathize, and even empathize. Thank You for showing me where to invest my time, energy, and resources in order to generate the largest return on my investment. Thank you for the perfect blueprint and divine intervention when I stray away from it. Father, forgive me for not always walking in the fullness of who You created me to be. Strengthen me for the nights when I am discouraged by how things are going. Give me a network of genuine and authentic supporters who can encourage me when sales are down. Don't allow money to ever be my sole motivation. Permeate my thoughts with the answer You desire me to share with the world and the motivation behind it. Let my "why" fuel all of my decisions moving forward. Teach me how and when to say, "No," knowing it is most important that I remain true to myself during this process. Show me how and when to pivot, so that my product or service remains relevant. Don't ever position me to have to choose between my peace and my profits. When decisions are necessary, strengthen my discernment, and let me always honor my purpose in You. Because of You, i am an entrepreneur.

In Jesus' name, Amen.

You seek color when everyone else is satisfied with black and white. You cut a hole in your shirt to make sure yours stands out from the crowd. You can't denote the exact measurements, but you know that a dash of this and a pinch of that will take the recipe from good to great. You possess an innate ability to think beyond the parameters of your current state of being, far pass the limitations and confinements of normalcy. You understand the difference between darkness and light. You adore their individual natures, but remain curious of how one immediately dispels the other. You have the spirit of your Father. You too are a creator.

You see, you're the one with the capacity to do, to construct, to establish, manufacture, develop, and design. The problem is, once upon a time, you convinced yourself otherwise. Maybe someone shunned your idea or embarrassed you because you asked a question. Perhaps, you tried it before and it didn't work. As a result, you then decided that was your cue from the universe that there was nothing left to be done. You gave up. You stopped trusting. You stopped believing. You stopped preparing. You stopped evolving. You stopped. You stepped away from purpose. You stepped away from God. You stepped away from you.

The beauty in our relationships with our Father is that He never leaves, even when we ask Him to or when we try to pretend He's not there. He never gives up on us, even when our lives are everything but an invitation for intimacy. All you have to do is invite Him back into your space. Revitalize your passions. Tap into your joy. Start writing again. Rehearse those lyrics. Tweak that recipe. Design that bag. Patent that product. Take those lessons. Research that investment. Submit that manuscript. Whatever you do, create.

Let us pray.

CONFESSION XXIV

i am A CREATIVE

Father, thank You for my ingenuity.

Thank You for endowing me with a spirit of curiosity and intrigue. Thank You for encouraging me to ask questions, to explore alternatives, to dream, and to imagine. Thank You for positioning me with a skill set that thrives off of analysis and innovation. Thank You for not always allowing me to accept things as they are, but being comfortable enough to dare to be different, to push the envelope, and to shatter glass ceilings. Thank you for showing me how to build the box or work around it. Thank You for teaching me how to think independently and surrounding me with others who appreciate that quality. Father, forgive me for not always walking in the fullness of who You created me to be. Don't allow life to drain me of my vigor, my excitement, my tenacity, or my zeal. Place me in environments where I can thrive as the embodiment and personification of manifestation. Open my eyes to see beyond the present moment. Train my mind to ask the next question, to seek quality responses, and to not let up until I am satisfied that You have nothing left for me to give or receive in that time and space. Incline my heart and mind to obey Your spirit at all times, to recognize when I'm on the verge of a discovery or invention that You want to produce, replicate, or refine. Don't allow me to downplay my virtuosity, my prowess, my gifts, my talents, or my genius to satisfy another's comfort level. Remind me that I am powerful beyond measure when I submit my ways to You. Engulf my life in continual experiences that inspire me to be more like You, the first creator. Because of You, i am a creative.

In Jesus' name, Amen.

Unfortunately, as you traverse through the narrow hills and vast valleys of life's expedition, trouble is inevitable, and more often than not, beyond your control. Accidents, illnesses, deaths, layoffs, abuse, racism, classism, discrimination, and soo much more abound in our midst. You are troubled on every side. Often times, it seems like the forces are against you, and the walls are closing in quicker and quicker by the day. You are broken, drowning in a sea of disappointment, gasping for air in each moment, wondering when will it all come to an end.

Sometimes, in your desperation for relief, you seek inappropriate solutions. You develop vices and addictions. You self-medicate using sex, drugs, or alcohol. You seek affirmation in all of the wrong places, giving your time, body, and attention to people, places, and circumstances that are not worthy of such an honor. You mistakenly look everywhere, to everyone, but God, for help.

There is nothing wrong with attempting to resolve your problem. The issue lies in your method or chosen practice. You're petitioning a powerless audience for assistance they never possessed the ability or capacity to give. Even with all of those mistakes, you're still able to start again, to do something different, to make a better decision. Your mistakes didn't disqualify you from His grace. Your shortcomings didn't eliminate the expected end He once promised you. All you have to do is remember who you are and whose you are. The rest will begin to fall back into place, one day, one moment, one second at a time.

Trust God. Trust yourself. Keep it moving. You are a queen. You are an overcomer. You can and you will triumph. Believe it. Memorize it. Recite it. Embody it. Then, go and do the doggone thing :).

Let us pray.

CONFESSION XXV

i am A CHAMPION

Father, thank You for placing a King inside of me.

Thank You for building the warrior within. Thank You for the victories I've won and the trials I've overcome. Thank You for the joy I feel as I conquer fear and perturbation. Thank You for my testimony that is energized and rejuvenated each time I share it with others. Thank You for not leaving me in times of conflict. Thank You for carrying me through the moments when I didn't have the strength or the desire to walk. Thank You for exchanging my burdens with Yours. Thank You for establishing a plan and a process that allowed me to learn and develop along the way. Thank You for the reassurance in Your word that reminds me that suffering with You guarantees that I will reign with You and that regardless of how things look, feel, or seem, You are on my team, so I cannot lose. Father, forgive me for not always walking in the fullness of who You created me to be. I am not naive enough to believe that things will always be great. I know that the enemy will continue to plot to steal, kill, and destroy anything that brings glory to Your name. I also know that you permit situations and circumstances to fortify my faith, enhance my endurance, and prepare me for whatever is to come next. Don't allow me to dissipate under the weight of the pressure You allow. Give me the proper perspective to accept the things I cannot change, to change the things I can, and the discernment to differentiate between the two extremes. Train my mind to see You in all situations, to look for the lesson so that my maturity can be expanded and enhanced. When I'm discouraged, doubting, stagnant, or complacent, propel me to keep going, knowing that in the end, I win. Because of You, i am a champion.

In Jesus' name, Amen.

Your mindset is just as important as your physical capabilities. In fact, some may argue that it's more important because it determines whether or not you will succeed. It's what feeds your willpower and motivation when you don't believe you can push forward any harder. You must always work to maintain a clear and healthy headspace.

Being mentally strong doesn't excuse or justify poor physical behaviors. As previously mentioned, your body is your temple. Like your spirit, its functionality is predicated upon what you feed it and how you nurture and care for it. Are you eating well? Are you participating in enjoyable activities? Are you getting enough sleep? Are you drinking water? When was the last time you felt energized?

These are some questions you need to ask yourself along with several others that delve into personal discovery. You are not allowed to dismiss personal care and development because times get challenging or relationships become difficult. Gluttony is not appropriate in any form. Self-control is necessary for stability, comfort, and continued prosperity.

Don't put wellness on the back-burner any longer. Stop telling yourself that you'll do it tomorrow or that it doesn't matter. It does. It matters because YOU MATTER! Take back control of whatever the thing is you have allowed to destruct any facet of your health. We all have areas of needed improvement. You can no longer neglect parts of you in the name of not having enough time, money, or even due to your efforts to care for others.

Believe that you can and eventually, you will. Make the changes, little by little, so that you can love what you see in the mirror and what you don't.

Let us pray.

CONFESSION XXVI

i am HEALTHY

Father, thank You for my life, my health, and my strength.

Thank You for Your peace that surpasses all understanding. Thank You for miracles and medicine, therapy and counseling, time, space, and opportunity that allows healing to dwell and flourish. Thank You for doctors and nurses, scientists and medical research, teachers and education, family and support systems, communities and joyful experiences. Thank You for love, one so deep and instinctively powerful that it can mend broken hearts, stabilize irrational emotions, soothe physical ailments, and calm unsettled minds. Thank You that Your blood still works and will never lose its power. Thank You for meeting me where I am, not expecting me to come to You with all of my problems solved and my messes cleaned up. Father, forgive me for not always walking in the fullness of who You created me to be. Remind me that You will never put more on me that I can bear. Teach me to ask for help when the weight seems to be to heavy to carry. Circumvent the strongholds of my thought pattern to align (or realign) them with how You view my illnesses, my ailments, and my weaknesses. Teach me how to properly identify my pain, from its root and at the source, so that I may seek the appropriate, holistic treatment, rather than soothing my symptoms with quick fixes and temporary balms. Show me the foods, drinks, and vitamins I should consume, and those I should stay away from. Filter my speech and my surroundings. Don't allow me to be ashamed of my sufferings, but to submit them to You for complete healing and total restoration. Continually show me that my mental, emotional, and spiritual health are just as important as my physical well-being. Let me always walk in the objective boldness of who I am in You. Because of You, i am healthy.

In Jesus' name, Amen.

Brokenhearted. Misunderstood. Abandoned. Discouraged. Angry. Frustrated. Triggered. We've all been there. In most cases, each word prompted the reflection of a certain incident, person, situation, or circumstance that hurt you, deeply. You never imagined they would do that to you. It never occurred to you that things wouldn't always be the way they once were. You didn't know you could shed that many tears. You weren't aware you could feel that type of pain or that it could linger this long.

In dealing with trauma, you must be honest with yourself. You must fully acknowledge how you are feeling and what initiated the pain. The most important part of the healing process is the diagnosis. Without properly zeroing in on the source of the issue, you can never fully and truly heal. Yes, you can ease or subdue or even partially tranquilize if you want to be extreme, but temporary solutions are fleeting and ultimately more detrimental in the long run. Contrary to popular belief, treating your symptoms won't actually heal your pain. It will simply distract you from its existence, which ultimately leaves it perfectly positioned to continue to grow and cause more damage.

In order to embody and maintain the life that you envision, you need to accept what God allows and tap into your inner strength. God doesn't expect you never to experience weakness. He simply asks you for a trade off, with Him, whenever it occurs. It's like hating what your mother packed for your lunch, but knowing you can switch lunches with a friend when you get to school. God is the friend. Give Him that bag! He will happily consume whatever you bring and exchange it for something you couldn't have prepared better yourself. Be healed and walk in your wholeness. It's yours for the taking.

Let us pray.

i am WHOLE

Father, thank You for mending my broken pieces.

Thank You for all of the things that make me uniquely me. Thank You for cleansing me of the situations, circumstances, and connections that attempted to rob me of my identity, my purpose, my vision, my sanity, my validity, and my truth. Thank You for placing people along my journey who value all of me, that encourage me to stand firm in my beliefs, and to embrace my individuality. Thank You for exposing my insecurities, so that I can address them, directly, and build a healthy self view. Thank You for my cocoon experiences that yielded a beautiful metamorphosis and released this butterfly into the freedom of flight and possibility that the air offers. Thank You for showing me how to overcome, how to fast and pray, how to live again. Father, forgive me for not always walking in the fullness of who You created me to be. When I am hurting, remind me that You are close to the brokenhearted. Help me understand that whatever it is, it's not the end of the world, just a trial or season I must endure but for a moment. Teach me to speak as You instruct, so that I can inspire others to be who You called them to be, unapologetically. When You prompt me to move, obliterate the rebellious nature within me. Saturate my actions in obedience, so that I can stay in Your will. I don't want to forget the lessons You've taught me or the experiences that brought me to this place. I simply want to be adamant and intentional about treasuring my positive outlook and maintaining a healthy mentality. Show me how to fully embrace life, yielding only to Your premonitions that are geared to protect me from hurt, harm, and danger. Help me to continuously embrace all of me, just the way You created me, beautiful and vibrant, fearfully and wonderfully made. Because of You, i am whole.

In Jesus' name, Amen.

Sometimes, you mess up. It wasn't the enemy. It wasn't your parents. It wasn't your siblings. It wasn't your spouse, your children, your coworkers, your boss, your neighbor, your friend, or your dog. It. Was. All. You. You knew the consequences. You knew the damage it could cause. You knew the potential heartbreak. You saw the signs. You ignored them. You heard the warnings. You disregarded them. You had a way out. You refused the exit. For whatever reason (low self-esteem, rejection, abandonment, vengeance, etc), you did it. You knew better and you still did it.

Here's the thing. We ALL make mistakes. We ALL trip up at some point. We ALL make bad decisions at one time or another. It's a part of the journey. It contributes to your evolution. You are not the anomaly. You are not the exception to the rule in this situation, and it's okay. Stop beating yourself up about it. Stop replaying the scenario. Stop triggering yourself. Accept it. Own it. Ask for forgiveness. And then, move on! God is not intimidated by your past, present, or future. He knew you'd mess up at some point, so He set a plan in motion long before you got here. Relax. Relate. Release.

If God is not pressed about your mistakes, why in creation are you tormenting yourself about them? Why forfeit your impact, your influence, and your future being stuck? Are you willing to throw everything away and risk it all based upon a memory? All that does is empower the moment to maintain its hold on you. Now, does that seem like the best decision you could make with all of the amazing goodness you have to offer the world? Stop. Think about it. Exactly. Nothing you can do separates you from the love, grace, and mercy of God. Be thankful and express your gratitude by wholeheartedly advocating for all of you, despite what you did and who you did it with.

Let us pray.

i am WORTHY

Father, thank You for taking a chance on me.

Thank You for traveling through unimaginable lows and irreplaceable highs with me. Thank You for crafting a life experience that only I could endure, overcome, and enjoy. Thank You for choosing me to invest your time, energy, and creativity. Thank You for granting me endless possibilities to succeed and excel. Thank You for exposing me to my truth and simultaneously teaching me how to accept it, all of it, even the parts that bring me discomfort, pain, disappointment, embarrassment, sadness, and fatigue. Thank You for continuously welcoming me into Your arms without judgment or condemnation. Thank You for correcting me in love, not leading with anger, and always granting me as many chances as I need to learn life lessons. Thank You for reminding me to recognize that despite my shortcomings, You are always there, ready, waiting, and willing to wrap me right back in Your embrace, until I am ready to try again. Thank You for not discrediting me, for not limiting my access, and for not restricting me from the bountiful abundance Your presence offers. Father, forgive me for not always walking in the fullness of who You created me to be. Don't ever let me take You or Your grace for granted. Continue to reassure me of my worthiness, by Your definition, removing the need for me to search for it elsewhere. As new insecurities arise, cloak them in Your blood and dismantle their ability to counteract the work You've already completed in and through me. Silence the voices of the naysayers and those who attempt to discourage me, especially when the loudest voice is mine. Teach me to ennoble myself with the same patience I'd extend to another, recognizing my value is not eradicated in the fall, but in my refusal to get back up again. Because of You, i am worthy.

In Jesus' name, Amen.

One of the purest gifts a child can offer is their innocence. In their world, there are no limitations, no boundaries, and no parameters. Nothing and no one can stop them. They trust anything and everything is possible simply because they haven't lived long enough to anticipate or expect otherwise. They don't need context or details. They simply believe. They have faith in people and circumstances that is not easily wavered. If you ask them their opinion on a matter, they don't discriminate. They give you a radical truth that may shock or even offend depending on the subject. Listening to them express their feelings is empowering and energizing, because it reminds you of the simple possibilities and potential of life.

Soo ... what happened during the transition between childhood and adulthood? Who robbed you of your dream? What negativity did you allow to consume your peace? What false narrative did you irresponsibly own as truth, so much so, your personal outlook and the lens, through which you view every situation, became jilted? When did you realize that only part of you was worthy of exposure and attention? What prompted you to start hiding, shrinking, and dialing back?

Whatever it was, whoever it was, whenever it was, read the following phrase very carefully, slowly, and repeatedly, if needed: It doesn't matter anymore. For too long, you have embodied a split persona, turning parts of you on and off, depending on your audience at the time. It no longer serves you to confine yourself to yourself. You deserve to live out loud, in the freedom of your childhood, to breathe without remorse, to flow in and out of spaces with your only priority being to fulfill the purpose God has entrusted to you. That's it. That's the assignment. That's the game.

You're welcome. Go forth and do great things.

Let us pray.

i am FREE

Father, thank You for releasing me to be me.

Thank You for saving me from iniquity, damnation, and hell. Thank You for restoring me from the bondage of my past and prior decisions. Thank You for shaping me beyond the expectations of others. Thank You for teaching me that I'm well within my rights to decline any relationship or opportunity that does not serve me in a way I can be proud of. Thank You for exposing me to positive perspectives and illuminated vision. Thank You for teaching me to accept the life You've given me, as it is, not to become overwhelmed or obsessed with morphing it into something You did not ordain. Thank You for showing me how to appreciate the small things and to savor the precious value authentic experiences offer. Thank You for forgiving me when I didn't know how to forgive myself. Thank You for healing me even when I couldn't express the magnitude of my pain. Thank You for teaching me about redemption, so I would not be selfish in offering it to others. Thank You for fashioning my taste for flavor, excitement, and spontaneity, for exposing me to joy, passion, and fulfillment. Thank You for binding all distractions and deterrences. Father, forgive me for not always walking in the fullness of who You created me to be. As I traverse amid the chaos and dysfunctions of life: racial tensions, political disparity, mental & physical illnesses, economic downturns, gender stereotypes, wealth discrimination, professional losses, and what seems to be a never-ending list of negative probabilities, show me how to hold tightly to Your word and Your hand. Regardless of what happens and when, never let me question the blessing and intrinsic treasure of my decision to align my life with You. Remind me that change is inevitable, but freedom is forever my choice. Because of You, i am free.

In Jesus' name, Amen.

Laughter is the greatest medicine. It is one of the most freeing expressions and enjoyable experiences we encounter on this side of glory. When you smile, there is a light that radiates from your inner being, illuminating your spirit for the eyes of those surrounding you. In that moment, you are releasing positive energy in such a way that it is felt in the vibrations of the room. Your victory resonates in such an intoxicating and exuberant manner that you rarely laugh alone. It triggers a similar reaction from others that seems to generate an invisible bridge between strangers, one that makes them feel like old friends or reunited family.

You deserve to be happy. You deserve to laugh. You deserve to smile. You deserve to enjoy your life. You are worthy of encounters that give you goosebumps and surprises that take your breath away. Your existence warrants occurrences that make you feel special, loved, appreciated, celebrated, and rejuvenated. You deserve to exhale. You deserve opportunities to release all of your inhibitions, dance like no one is watching, sing to the top of your lungs, and laugh until you have tears in your eyes, are barely breathing, and couldn't compose a proper sentence if you tried.

Quite frankly, you deserve the best God has to offer, so He gave you just that. The caveat is that you have to embrace it. You have to avail yourself to internalize your joy in such a way that you're willing to do any and everything it takes to protect it, at all costs.

Fight for it. Enjoy it. The joy that you have is special. The world didn't give it, and the world cannot, shall not, dare not take it away.

Let us pray.

i am HAPPY

Father, thank You for joy unspeakable.

Thank You for victory. Thank You for laughter. Thank You for passion. Thank You for celebration. Thank You for precious memories. Thank You for salvation. Thank You for direct communication with and access to You. Thank You for the embrace of a loved one and the twinkle in the eye of a child. Thank You for scents that trigger positive thoughts and experiences that remind me of my progress and transformation. Thank You for the sounds of music and the melodies that reverberate within my soul. Thank You for clear blue skies and cozy rainy days. Thank You for elevation and advancement. Thank You for family and friends, coworkers and community. Thank You for challenges that strengthen my character and fortify my integrity. Father, forgive me for not always walking in the fullness of who You created me to be. As I reflect on the innumerable facets of my human experience, those that have shaped my optimism and curated my compassion, teach me how to remain grateful. In the depths and crevices of ineffable suffering, allow me to pause, breathe, reflect, and release. Remind me of better moments and greater times. Keep me cognizant that gratitude changes perspective, so if I can think better, I can be better. Even as I strive to unveil what's next, what else I can offer, and how I can positively impact those around me, don't allow me to become blind to circumstances and suffering that is not my own. Keep me sensitive to Your spirit and to the needs of those around me. Show me how to balance my happiness with a sincere and authentic desire to contribute to the happiness of others. When all else fails, remind me of the never-ending value of my smile, and most importantly, everyone and everything that contributes to it. Because of You, i am happy.

In Jesus' name, Amen.

It is the most beautiful expression we can convey to another. It embodies courage, faith, wisdom, strength, patience, gratitude, forgiveness, kindness, humility, peace, style, charisma, and joy. It penetrates the deepest parts of our being. It drives us to listen, to learn, and to live. It is an example, a standard, an expectation, and an exploration all at once. It encourages. It sacrifices. It serves. It soothes. It heals.

It is both the easiest, most natural expression we have; yet, often the most difficult to understand and demonstrate. It is not just what we are called to do and to receive, it is who we are called to be. It refines. It purifies. It sustains. It stabilizes. It lifts. It pushes. It pulls. It propels. It settles. It is selfless and honorable, timeless and digestible, savory and delectable, faithful and irreplaceable.

It's the gift we never asked for, but were precious enough to receive and dare not fathom living without. It's the reward for our existence and the key to eternity. It transcends. It elevates. It inspires. It appreciates. It submits. It dominates. It is the greatest creation beyond the human being itself. It is everything we need and everything we could ever desire.

It is you. It is me. It is God.

It is love.

It is yours. Take it. Cherish it. Embrace it. Exude it. Give it, freely, often, consistently, to Him, to yourself, to others. It is your duty, your obligation, your responsibility, and your honor to be able to do so. Never forget its power. Never deny its access. Never refute its capabilities. Never leave home without it.

Let us pray.

CONFESSION XXXI

i am LOVED

Father, thank You for being You.

It's in You I live, in You I move, and in You I have my being. It's because of You that I even know what love is, what it does, and why it means anything to me at all. When You had a choice, You chose the ultimate sacrifice for no other reason than that of love. You are simultaneously the epitome of its definition, the personification of its beauty, and the embodiment of the standard it upholds. You removed all excuses for misunderstanding its purpose and its value before I was born. You guaranteed that I had everything I needed to replicate Your behavior when You created me in Your image. You left instructions to ensure that I didn't limit or restrict it to myself, but rather, I remain intentional about sharing it with those around me. You identified it as the distinguishing factor between those of us who know You and those who need to be introduced. Thank You. Thank You for Your contributions that shaped how I perceive love, receive love, and express love. Thank You for engulfing my life with an unexplainable gem that can only be experienced to be appreciated; yet, is truly most beneficial when its reciprocated. Father, forgive me for not always walking in the fullness of who You created me to be. Forgive me for not remembering You in my thoughts, words, and deeds, in my communications, expressions, and actions. Remind me that sharing Your love is my greatest assignment. Beyond loving You and myself, it is what matters most and what You are depending on me to do on a daily basis. God, when I lose my way and I'm choosing to withhold the one thing You purposed me to give away, allow me to look to You. If I seek Your face and not Your hand, because of Your love, I will be rewarded with the treasures of both. Thank You. Because of You, i am loved.

In Jesus' name, Amen.

When it's all over, what do you want the world to remember about you? Who will men say you were? Are you preparing to leave a legacy you're proud of or have you succumb to a persona that is actually the antithesis of the one you're aiming to etch into history?

Today, right now, in this moment, you must remember that you are God's greatest. Your existence is a testament to His love for you and His belief in your ability to do amazing things. He had other options. He still does; yet, He has not taken His hand off of your life. He has not forgotten about you or forsaken you. He has never left you and He has no intentions to start now.

In order to establish yourself as the epitome of His divine creation, you must become everything He had in mind when He formed you.

It's not as complicated as you think.

Stand in the totality of who you are. Embrace your flaws and your fabulousness. Use adversity as the fuel that pushes you towards your next destination. Resist invitations to tear down others and certainly refrain from destroying yourself. Believe in your significance. Believe in your dreams again. Eliminate all of the negativity that rests inside you. Divorce yourself from the trauma, the hardships, the defeats, and the brokenness.

Your time is now. Your ability to excel is here. Your window of opportunity has arrived. The door to the life you were destined to live is open. Walk through it just as you are, unapologetically and authentically, boldly and confidently. Be crazy in love with yourself and let everyone else follow suit.

Let us pray.

i am ENOUGH

Father, thank You for validating all of me.

Thank You for seeing me worthy of Your investment into my creation. Thank You for choosing to love every part of me, even the parts I didn't originally love myself. Thank You for teaching me how to properly evaluate myself and my circumstances through Your lens of value, merit, and understanding. Thank You for reminding me that comparison is often the thief of joy, peace, and a healthy perspective, particularly when it is absent of You. Thank You for crafting a heart filled with gratitude inside of me that allows me to appreciate people, places, things, and myself as they are, not as I believe they should be. Thank You for removing the expectations that blindly set me up for disappointment, frustration, and failure. Thank You for instilling in me a vision to serve Your people using everything You've given me. Father, forgive me for not always walking in the fullness of who You created me to be. When I doubt I can continue on this journey, fortify my faith. When I question if You made the right decision in choosing me, enlighten my wisdom. When I'm fearful of what lies ahead of me, renew my courage. When I'm hesitant to make the right decision, strengthen my discernment. When I'm losing myself in the midst of those around me, elevate my confidence. When I'm becoming weary in well doing, rejuvenate my perseverance. When I'm lonely and spiraling in a cycle of torment and depression, activate my support system. When I'm confused about the results or the circumstances surrounding me, infiltrate my thought pattern. When I think I can't, remind me that with You, in You, and for You, I always can. Because of You, i am enough.

In Jesus' name, Amen.

The secret has been revealed. You are free to be everything you desire because you are His and He is yours. Unleash every morsel of your magic into the Earth. The world has been waiting on you, the complete you, and there is no reason to rob it of the fullness of your presence any longer.

You and you alone determine how you show up and what message you convey.

Parts of you will change. Ideas will morph. Expectations will evolve. What must remain consistent is your devotion, your commitment, your determination, and your willingness to accept all of you, all of the time, the good, the bad, the ugly, the indifferent, and everything in between.

Can you do that?

Evolution is a decision. If you want to become, to transform, to leave behind patterns and bad habits in order to discover what's on the other side, you're going to have to do something different. It takes courage. It requires ambition. More than anything, it yearns for acceptance of truth, the whole truth, and nothing but the truth.

Truth is and always has been the answer. It's really the only safe ground to stand upon. You deserve honesty. You simply have to remember to give it to yourself first. God's opinion and yours are the only two that matter and His mind has already been made up. He is waiting on you to accept your truth, own it, and then use it as the glue you need to hold your newfound life together.

Let us pray.

CONFESSION XXXIII

i am THE OTHER WOMAN

Father, I come to You as humbly as I know how, thanking You for this day I have never seen before, and will never see again.

Thank You for allowing me to discover, respect, and refine the other parts of who I am. Thank You for turning my wailing into dancing, for giving me beauty for ashes. Thank You for birthing in me a reverence for my acceptance, for reminding me that self-rejection holds no allure. Father, forgive me for not always walking in the fullness of who You created me to be. Because of You, i am saved. Because of You, i am chosen. Because of You, i am faithful. Because of You, i am gracefully broken. Because of You, i am not crazy. Because of You, i am secure. Because of You, i am patient. Because of You, i am intelligent. Because of You, i am powerful. Because of You, i am beautiful. Because of You, i am sensual & sexual. Because of You, i am a daughter. Because of You, i am a sister. Because of You, i am a wife. Because of You, i am a mother. Because of You, i am a friend. Because of You, i am an intercessor. Because of You, i am a servant. Because of You, i am a student. Because of You, i am an educator. Because of You, i am a professional. Because of You, i am an entrepreneur. Because of You, i am a creative. Because of You, i am a champion. Because of You, i am healthy. Because of You, i am whole. Because of You, i am worthy. Because of You, i am happy. Because of You, i am free. Because of You, i am loved. Because of You, i am enough. Because of You, I can embrace every facet of my existence, explore every crevice of my opportunities, and do anything and everything You ask me to do. Because of You, i am a masterpiece.

Thank You for creating me just the way I am.

In Jesus' name, Amen.

Hey you!

I see you where YOU are, in the perfect place to gather your inside things and get to BEing. If you were anything like me while immersing myself in this work, "*i am The Other Woman*," I felt like I was in the middle of a grassy field, just me and Teira, musing. The words leapt off of the pages, allowing me to feel with expressions of tears. It was like, "YES, I finally have language for these inarticulate feelings. SHWHEW!" Big exhale.

The perspectives of our lives that are sometimes left wanting, I now feel empowered to address through the practical solutions and the prayers in this book. Teira provided gentle reminders of how important it is for us to be intentional about valuing ourselves, our voices, our assignments, our words, even while they are still in formation. This work challenged me to embrace more the dichotomy of me that houses me, *The Other Woman*. I see now, the beautiful creation of music my life writes bringing sweet melody to the world. This work is beautiful, lovely, dynamic, and soul filling.

NOW, where do we go from here? How do we offer ourselves space and time to get to know and love more of *The Other Woman*? How do we give life to her, realizing her desires and idiosyncrasies? How do we love her into living?

First.
STOP. BE. BREATHE.
Intentionally take time to sit with yourself, embracing how alive you are right now. Our presentness is important in realizing our innate value to ourselves. Be present for yourself, intentionally.

Then.
Evaluate your space.
Who's in it? Who belongs? Who's making valuable contributions? Who's sucking up your necessary daily deposits of joy and peace?
Cleanse your space. Embrace peace. Be alive. Live.

Moving forward.
Create a life for discovery and growth.
The Other Woman deserves a chance to thrive. Consistently inquire within yourself, "What makes me alive? What makes me sing? What makes me dance?" Answer yourself. Curate ideal days that make space for this. Your days turn into weeks. Your weeks turn into months. Your months turn into Full Throttle Living ... a life you enjoy, brimming over with purpose.

- Jametta Chandler Moore

"Our Father which art in heaven, Hallowed be thy name. Thy kingdom come, Thy will be done in earth, as it is in heaven. Give us this day our daily bread. And forgive us our debts, as we forgive our debtors. And lead us not into temptation, but deliver us from evil: For thine is the kingdom, and the power, and the glory, for ever. Amen."

- ***The Lord's Prayer****, Matthew 6:9-13, KJV*

NOTES

1. Williamson, M. 1992. *A Return to Love.* New York: HarperCollins

www.ingramcontent.com/pod-product-compliance
Lightning Source LLC
Chambersburg PA
CBHW050704160426
43194CB00010B/1988